NORMAL

How Our Chase Towards Living an Ordinary Life Gets in the Way of Our Extraordinary Life

SARAH GIFFORD

This book is dedicated to **you.**

Not the you that you think you should be.
Not the you that you were told you should be.

This book is dedicated to the **you** *in which you feel so at peace, so secure, and so natural.*

Table of Contents (table of tools)

Introduction

In 2004, Memorial Day weekend promised beautiful weather, and the school year was nearing an end. This meant that the long weekend consisted primarily of bouncing around from friend's house to friend's house until someone's mom called someone's mom and called us home for the night. That Saturday night, however, was different. I was preparing for that call to head back home, which I was quite honestly ready for after such a long and fun day out and about, but instead a friend suggested a sleepover.

Instantly, a debate stirred inside of me. I did not want to sleep over. I knew that all of my other friends jumped at this invite and I wanted to want to take part, but nothing sounded better to me than heading home and meeting back up with everyone tomorrow. But, as I mentioned, I knew that I *should* want to, that it was normal for 3rd graders to love sleepovers, so I agreed.

'Everyone my age/in my grade/on the planet loves sleepovers, why can't I just be normal and like them?' This was the inner monologue that went through my brain that evening when I was picked up, in tears, at about 11pm, after yet another failed sleepover attempt.

I start with this example to paint a bit of a picture of how I perceived my feelings and my emotions at that time in my life. I was convinced that no one else was struggling the way that I was, and that mindset was dangerous. That mindset followed me through elementary, middle, and high school, through college, and beyond. I just now am feeling like I have the confidence to talk myself out of this mindset when it creeps back in, but it is something that I work at often.

Every single person has a story. We have all been through unique experiences that have challenged us, shaped us, and ultimately taught us. I am writing this piece as a 25 year old reflecting upon my story so far. I had been thinking for a while why I (and most people I know, really) struggle through periods in life. Why do we make things harder than they need to be? As I have gotten older I have started to feel the desire to understand the *why* behind social norms and other aspects of life that are expected.

I simply got tired of doing things just because that's the way it was done, and because that's what I had been conditioned to desire throughout my upbringing. I by no means have the answer to this existential question, but I do know that we put a lot of undue stress on this concept of 'normalcy'. We feel as if we need to enjoy certain things, have certain goals and ambitions, etc. in order to be 'normal'.

As I've been thinking about how I got to where I am today and what experiences shaped me into this person, I realized that my chasing 'normal' made my quest for joy and happiness much harder than necessary.

This book is separated out into chapters, or "tools" that I have learned through lessons over the years. These tools are things that have helped me become who I am today and have helped me navigate through some serious anxiety and self—doubt. I will say that some of this book is somewhat self—serving, in that I wrote it as a form of self reflection, a way to see some of the things I've overcome, and how I have changed through some of my hardest times. I do think that others may find this helpful and relatable, as well, though.

Each chapter will encompass some tool, or skill, that I've found helpful through my life so far. Within these chapters, I'll delve deep into what this looks like in real life and why I think that specific tool and skill is so important. At the end of each chapter, I'll provide you with an actionable takeaway and 'instructions' as to how to take these skills into your daily life. Together, we'll build the most robust, well rounded, and bold tool belts that we'll wear with confidence.

Some of these chapters will be long and include stories to speak to the chapter's goal. Some of these chapters will be incredibly succinct, quick, and to the point. I am not a natural writer, but I am a natural story teller. This writing may be choppy and all over the place, but that's me! Some of the pieces in this book are lighthearted, fun advice, and some are heavier reminders and pieces of advice. I'm just a girl who has been through some hard spaces and times, and I want to help you navigate these times for yourself.

I'm writing this book because I know that I needed this book as a middle schooler, high schooler, college student, and heck I still need it now. I'm writing this book so that somewhere, someone who is struggling with similar issues I worked through can read this and remind themselves, 'Hey, I'm not alone. This is hard as heck but I'm not alone.'

1
Knowledge & Confidence

One Friday evening, in the fall of 2014, I was just coming off of a busy school week and was happily enjoying a low key evening of catching up from the week, Netflix, and most likely ice cream (choco chip cookie dough FTW). This was just what I needed, I knew it, but there was a block and I was struggling to allow myself to enjoy it.

"I just wish you'd be more like a normal 19 year old, that's all." This phrase was said to *me* by *myself*. I was confident that although this evening may be what I wanted, it was not what a 'normal' 19 year old was to be doing on Friday and Saturday nights, therefore I was not normal.

Throughout my childhood, and truly into early adulthood, I was convinced that I was not 'normal' for needing and craving alone time. I was convinced that I was unlikable and just odd for preferring this to going out with friends every weekend. It simply wasn't what I wanted to do, but I felt confident that I should want that.

This grave disparity between what I wanted to need and what I actually needed caused a great deal of anxiety, uncertainty, and self—doubt. As I explained earlier, my inner monologue usually consisted of me putting myself down for not being 'normal', for wanting to do other things with my time than that of what I was seeing other classmates doing. The truth of the matter was, though, that I would never have put anyone else down for these things. Why was I being *so* hard on myself for something that I would admire and envy in someone else?

Shifting gears a bit, I want to tell you a story about a friend of mine who let this mindset become her mantra. This friend of mine was so, so excited for high school. She could not wait to get to her locker and decorate it and of course organize it just to her liking. She played field hockey, and spent time at open fields over the summer with teammates, new and old. She went to pick up her textbooks and class schedule and was buzzing with excitement. She was going to be normal.

The first day of high school came and went, seemingly without a hitch. She found her classes no problem, and really liked her teachers. In my friend's high school, freshmen start school one day before the rest of the high school, to allow the newcomers to navigate through the school and figure out things like classroom locations, locker locations, bathroom locations, etc. without having the stress of those *monstrous* other high schoolers.

The second day of high school, when all of the other high schoolers joined in on the fun, was much different than the first. She couldn't help but compare and feel like she wasn't like her other classmates, freshmen or anyone else. She thought this would just be a quick feeling — typical jitters as she adjusted to the new school. She went to field hockey practice that night, still feeling a bit off.

When she woke up the next morning, now on day three of this school year, it became very apparent to her — she simply could not go to school. She sat in the passenger seat of her parent's car and bawled. She could not pinpoint what it was, and neither could her parents, but she was not able to get out of the car and walk into the school. Sure, she was physically fine, but the thought of walking in those doors and through those hallways made her feel sick to her stomach. She refused to go in.

In talking this over with my friend, and looking back at this now, she truly wishes she had more insight into why she felt this way. Thinking about this situation logically, she had absolutely nothing to be nervous or scared about. As I mentioned, she knew her class locations, had some good friends, had great teachers. Check, check, check — why was she feeling this way? That's the thing about anxiety and feelings in general, sometimes it's hard to separate the logical from the emotional. She still can't pinpoint why she was feeling this way, but there was an uneasiness deep down that was speaking louder than logic was.

Unsure about how to react and respond to this situation, her parents took her home from school without dropping her off, and went up to her room and wept. 'Why are you doing this to yourself?' 'Why can't you just be normal?' 'Kids love high school, why can't you be normal like them and just go?' Here was her inner monologue creeping in, like an unwelcome house guest.

While my friend was calming down, or trying to, her parents had reached out to her guidance counselor at the school. Nothing like introducing yourself by way of "Hey, nice to meet you! Our daughter is refusing to come to school and she's upstairs weeping, any thoughts?"

To this day, she is not 100% sure how that conversation went down, but she was informed that she would be going to school tomorrow. There it was again, the panic. The tears. The uneasy feeling. Her parents had talked with the guidance counselor, and they were all three going to go talk with her first thing in the morning about how to sort through this.

Some way or another, that alarm clock buzzed in the morning, and it was time to head to day 4 of high school. The three of them walked to the guidance counselor's office, she was in tears, and they sat down. In her mind, at the time, the only thing that would ever

solve this was for her to be homeschooled. Truly. Again, she could not pinpoint exactly what made her feel so incredibly anxious, uneasy, and simply miserable, but she was convinced that the only way to combat this feeling was to run away and finish high school at home.

In this meeting, the four of them re—worked her school schedule to allow her to start each day, all of 1st period, in the guidance counselor's office. At the time, this seemed little help, as she was positive she would be miserable all day and postponing that feeling for a mere 53 minutes would do little to subside this. However, she reluctantly agreed to give this a shot.

The next few weeks, unfortunately, were more of the same. Having the ability to start each day in the guidance counselor's office was incredibly helpful for my friend, as she was oftentimes able to pull herself back from the downward spiral she was heading by 2nd period. For about the first month of the school year, about 3 of the 5 days of each week, my friend's dad had to walk her into the school and into the counselor's office. This was simply because she refused to get out of the car.

Looking back, what compounded and made this so hard was that she truly believed that she was not 'normal'. She truly believed that every single person that walked by, every person who did not have their dad walking them into the counselor's office, was 'normal' and here she was, yet again, confirming everyone's suspicions that she was not apart of that category. This belief held so closely made her underlying anxiety/nervousness/fears that much more of a burden. She was unbelievably mad at herself for feeling this way, and that anger only festered.

Here is the kicker to this story — this friend I just told you all about, ***it's me.*** That is my story of how I started high school.

I have come a long way since those hard, dark days of my freshman year of high school. I am incredibly proud of the person I have become and am becoming through these experiences.

Looking back at this experience and others, I can say undoubtedly that I am able to really recognize & acknowledge myself and what I need. Not only is this self awareness imperative, but with it comes the *confidence* to act upon it and to control it. This is something that I know I will never *truly* master. But I have come so far in this knowledge and skillset through my struggles.

I am what I would consider to be an extroverted introvert, in that I "recharge" by spending time alone. I know that I am a person who loves to be around people but also needs some serious alone time to recharge. I know that I am a person who likes to feel wanted, respected, and validated. I know that I am a person who enjoys most weekend nights at home alone, and I know that I am a person who thoroughly enjoys that. It has taken me almost a quarter of a century to be able to say that confidently.

Put it in your tool belt

I challenge you, right now, to use the space below, and make a list like this of your own. I'll help you get started.

I know that I am a person who..

I know that I am a person who..

I know that I am a person who..

I know that I am a person who..

I know that I am a person who..

I know that I am a person who..

2
Social Media

Truthfully, I love social media. I also hate social media. I am a firm believer that used correctly, social media can be a great tool for inspiration, community, growth, and more. However, I was not quite this wise when I was a mere 20 years old, and I was following/admiring the people that I thought I should be following. I was following the people that most people my age followed, because that was normal. Looking back now, I have no doubt that my following certain people on social media made my life much harder than it needed to be. This is certainly by no fault of theirs, but I was following people who were doing the things I thought I should be doing.

While I was enjoying a night of Netflix or reading, I would scroll through and see people going out for the third night that week. I was happily studying alone in a coffee shop when I stopped to scroll and came across a picture of people studying with friends in the library. In most of these instances, I was happy and fine doing my own thing until I wasn't. Until I was reminded that I should be more normal, that I should be doing these activities with friends. That I should be wanting to do these things. Queue the inner monologue!

Writing this now, I am still in my early twenties and by no stretch of the imagination have things figured out, but I do know one thing for certain. Who we follow on social media can make an entire world of difference.

I have become incredibly particular about who I follow and who I allow to follow me, and that has made all of the difference. I use social media as a way to feel inspired and energized, instead of as a means to compare. I challenge you, the next time you see something on your feed that makes you feel bad about yourself, to press "unfollow". It's the easiest thing to do!

Put it in your tool belt

For this actionable activity, all that I want you to do is notice how you're feeling the next few times you log onto social media, and take note of it. I challenge you to describe your mood after scrolling through socials, and as you unfollow uninspiring accounts & find accounts that you resonate with, take notice of how that affects your mood.

Today...
Today, after scrolling through social media, I feel...

A week or so later...
Today, after scrolling through social media, I feel...

A week or so later...
Today, after scrolling through social media, I feel...

A week or so later...
Today, after scrolling through social media, I feel...

A week or so later...
Today, after scrolling through social media, I feel...

A week or so later...
Today, after scrolling through social media, I feel...

A week or so later...
Today, after scrolling through social media, I feel...

3

Maturity

This is one of the skills that is harder to learn and master, but is oh, so important. This is a skill that has taken me a quarter of a century to harness and I still struggle through often. This skill is the maturity to remind myself that however I'm feeling is *okay*.

So many times, I know that I have only worsened my anxious spirals by beating myself up and telling myself the lies that these feelings are not normal. Now, this is not to say that it's ok to allow ourselves to sit in these head—spaces, but giving yourself the grace and permission to work through and past these feelings is incredibly powerful and rewarding.

I think that one of the worst things we can do for ourselves is try to force ourselves out of a funk or of a hard period in our lives. Whether it's after a hard breakup, a hard day at work, friend troubles, or whatever it may be, it is *healthy* to feel all the feelings after these things. As I mentioned in the earlier paragraph, though, what is not okay is allowing ourselves to *stay* in that hard place in our lives.

As cliche as it may sound, there is real freedom in getting feelings and thoughts off of your chest and verbalizing these to another person. This process looks different to everyone, also, which is so cool! This may mean talking to a therapist, this may mean talking with a friend, this may mean writing a book, this may mean talking to Siri on your phone. Just talk it out! I promise. My challenge for you, in the next few weeks, is to find an outlet for yourself. Find some way to get all of your thoughts and feelings out.

I have been through some hard and dark times throughout my life, and there have been times that I didn't think the dark cloud would ever shift. Guess what, though. It did! When I'm having a hard day, or a hard week, or heck, I've had hard months before, I am starting to realize that although these periods of life suck, it's okay.

When in doubt, remember this. **You have made it through 100% of your bad days**. However that looked, if you are reading this book, you have made it out the other side of even your hardest time in life. That's saying something, and it shows that you feel all the feelings. I'm really proud of you for that.

Put it in your tool belt

Over the course of the next few weeks and months, I challenge you to observe yourself, your thoughts, and actions, as you come across and work through hard times. Take note of how you were feeling, how you reacted, and what helped you get through these times. Reminder: it is okay to say that what you did to get through a hard time was to just 'feel it out & let it pass'.

What happened?

How did you feel and/or how did you react?

What helped?

What happened?

How did you feel and/or how did you react?

What helped?

What happened?

How did you feel and/or how did you react?

What helped?

What happened?

How did you feel and/or how did you react?

What helped?

4
Evaluate 'Should'

One of the things that I feel has, in the past, held me back from appreciating all that I do have in life is that I feel like I should have something different. I am doing this thing, and I challenge you to try it with me, in which I stop and ask myself 'why?' And really working to get to the root of why I'm feeling pressured to do something whenever I notice myself saying the s word (should) to myself. Here's an example scenario.

New Years Eve. Coworkers and friends and family are all talking about how they are going out and it's going to be a wild night. Honestly, I wanted nothing more than a cozy night in and to start the new year well rested, ha! But I found myself saying "Sarah you *should* go out, you *should* want to go out" and so on and so forth.

It wasn't until I really got to the root of why I was feeling the way I was, that I began to realize that my motivations for 'wanting' to want to do something were purely extrinsic. Once I began delving deep into the motive behind my feeling like I have to be doing a certain thing or acting a certain way, I began to realize a pattern. I am realizing that my motivation for these types of feelings lies within my desire to be 'normal', as if my craving of that cozy night in was something no one else ever wanted.

There is a lot to be said about where our motivation comes from. I eluded to this in the last paragraph, and I debated making this an entire tool chapter! However, this ties in so well with our inner 'shoulds' that I want to mention it here. When we're entering into a

new venture — be that professionally or personally — our motivation for overcoming hurdles and facing challenges is either of the intrinsic or extrinsic nature. We can be intrinsically motivated by challenges because we love how it makes us feel to accomplish that particular task. Generally, for example, people join pick—up volleyball games simply for the joy that we harness from playing a fun game with friends, not for the prize or trophy.

Extrinsic motivation, by contrast, indicates that there is something of external value that we are hoping to win or achieve by completing the task. On the surface, at least, we complete assignments in school for the *grade*. We do not want to be reprimanded by not completing an assignment, and we are motivated to submit a satisfactory assignment by the prospect of a good grade. That value we are placing in completing that assignment is external.

I believe that this concept of extrinsic vs. intrinsic motivation can be applied to our motives outside of the school or professional setting, though, too. Every time we are saying to ourselves that we want to do something because it's what we're supposed to do, think about where that motivation is coming from. Are you motivated to do something you don't want to do because you want recognition and praise for being 'normal'?

Right now is where I need to put a big DISCLAIMER in red in this book. There is immense power and positive experience in getting out of your comfort zone. I do not say any of these things to urge you to be or to stay small and in control of every single piece of your life. I want you to go out and be the very best version of yourself, whatever that may look like. That often *requires* that we get uncomfortable with our narrative that we're telling ourselves. I have a hard question for you all, but I know you can handle it. What if your comfort zone is succumbing to external values (extrinsic motivation)? What if your comfort zone is pushing your true desires to the back burner? What if getting out of your comfort zone implies having real, honest, and sometimes hard, conversations with ourselves?

There have been many situations throughout my life in which I've had to sit back and ask myself "Sarah. *Why* do you want these things? What is the motivation behind being so gung—ho about this?" For me, it has been dating.

BAZINGA there it is. We knew it was going to come up in this book at some point, didn't we? Truthfully, this is where my thinking about motivation arose from. I sometimes felt (and still do!) like there is some sort of race to get into a relationship, to get married, to have kids, etc. This was a race that I was *unquestionably* losing. I beat myself up constantly about this.

The lies I told myself about dating can make me cry, and they did. I wanted to be worthy enough for a relationship. I wanted to prove that I was worthy. I realized at some point in my early to mid 20s that my motivation for wanting these things was purely extrinsic.

Here's another DISCLAIMER for you. Evaluating your should and your motivation are *amazing* tools (in my humble opinion) to determine what you truly want in life. Please, please, please, though, don't think that these are 'get out of struggle free' cards. These are not mindsets we normally find ourselves in. It takes a conscious effort to remind yourself to think about these things, and to evaluate these things. It should come as *no* surprise to anyone that I still fall into what I like to call 'funky spirals'. The key, though, is recognizing that and making the conscious effort to reframe your thinking.

Put it in your tool belt

This strategy/practice can be applied to so many situations, too. The next time you catch yourself saying something along the lines of 'I should be ...', stop there! Stop and ask yourself why you feel this way. What is the motivation behind you feeling like you need to be acting or performing or living a certain way? I can say confidently that in the majority of situations, the cause is somehow related to how you feel the decision to do what you *want* to do will be perceived.

My Narrative	*Question (why?)*	*Answer*
I should want to go out to the bars on NYE.	*Why do I feel like wanting to go out is important?*	*It's what everyone else is doing so I have to.*

My Narrative	Question (why?)	Answer

5
Be Picky

I consider it one of the biggest blessings in my life that I have people around me who I can go to for guidance. I do not take that lightly — I am deeply thankful to have those in my life who have gone through struggles from which I can learn. One of the things that I have learned, however, through my adventure on this earth so far, is that there is not one single person who has been on the exact journey that you have.

As I said above and in previous chapters, there is immense power in talking through hurdles we're faced with and how we plan to surmount said hurdles, but I challenge you to take your own advice first. Not one person other than you can provide guidance while taking into account the emotional *and* the logical elements of your scenario.

One of the things that I have noticed is that I have a (very subconscious) habit of prioritizing other people's thoughts/ideas/opinions about my choices above my own. Once I realized this and really accepted that this was something I was doing, and was really self—sabotaging myself by doing so, I became determined to work on lasting and sustainable habits to counteract this. Turns out, unfortunately, that this isn't a habit that we can simply turn on and off. In order to make the sustainable change to asking yourself advice first, it requires some level of self—examination and self—reflection.

The good news here is that while it may take time to bring this subconscious habit to the conscious brain, the process is quite simple. All I am asking you to do, next time you're faced with a decision, is to think through what you would like to do. Informally, what is your gut telling you? Take this into account while also asking others what they think.

Every situation will look different, but I do challenge you to take your gut inclination into account more than the others'. Warning: this will feel uneasy at first. You very well may feel like you're disappointing people because you're not following their advice. This is okay to feel this way! The best thing to do is to acknowledge those uneasy feelings and remind yourself, 'These feelings are here because I am not used to following my own intuition. I am growing.'

Put it in your tool belt

Just as I mentioned above, I challenge you to really examine where your unsteadiness surrounding making a final decision. The simple act of asking ourselves this question can be life changing — again, this tendency to go with what others want us to do can be entirely subconscious at times!

The Decision I'm Faced With:

What Do I Want To Do?

Is my hesitation based upon others' opinions, or is there another factor playing into my hesitation?

The Decision I'm Faced With:

What Do I Want To Do?

Is my hesitation based upon others' opinions, or is there another factor playing into my hesitation?

The Decision I'm Faced With:

What Do I Want To Do?

Is my hesitation based upon others' opinions, or is there another factor playing into my hesitation?

The Decision I'm Faced With:

What Do I Want To Do?

Is my hesitation based upon others' opinions, or is there another factor playing into my hesitation?

6
Recognize Your Superpower

I haven't met you (although I hope to someday!) but if you're anything like me, you have always been told that you feel too much. Maybe you've been told that you're too empathetic. Maybe, also, you've been told that you are too susceptible to take on emotions, good or bad, of others around you. I am going to challenge these statements, though. What if, and stay with me here, what if our ability to feel so deeply alongside others, is one of the greatest gifts?

What if our ability to understand others' emotions is a superpower? If anything, I am inclined to believe that this makes us acutely more aware of our profound influence on others around us. In thinking through how much we are able to take on, emotionally, by others, why in the world would we not want to turn around and emit as much positivity, light, and brightness as possible?

I have another disclaimer for you here, though. In my 25 years of life, I have come to (quickly) realize that there will always be negative emotions to take on in the world around us. As unfortunate as this sounds, it is simply the truth. Knowing this, though, my challenge for you is to make it a point to not only feel empathetic towards those hurting, but to also share in the joy & the happiness of the world, as well. It may not seem like it sometimes, but there truly is *so much* joy to be found in the world.

Put it in your tool belt

The next time you're feeling extreme emotions as a result of taking on others' emotions, let's explore that! It's important to recognize where these feelings are coming from, and to acknowledge that these are emotions we're feeling from an external source.

The emotion I'm feeling right now	What has prompted me to feel this way?	Is this an emotion that I have taken on from someone else?

The emotion I'm feeling right now	What has prompted me to feel this way?	Is this an emotion that I have taken on from someone else?

7
Make Gratitude a Habit

I don't know about you, but when I see an author or a blogger say something like, 'Gratitude is the key to happiness! Just be grateful for what you **do** have!!' I tend to get upset. Ironic, isn't it, then, that this chapter is literally all about gratitude? Here is my take on integrating gratitude into your daily routine, while also understanding that simply focusing on the good things won't make the hard moments go away.

In the fall of 2020, I became plagued with the some of the most intense anxiety attacks I have ever experienced. I struggled to pinpoint exactly what was triggering these — maybe it was all of 2020, maybe it was my turning 25, maybe it was all of the above. However, I couldn't deny the fact that I was not in a good place. I would argue that going through this experience was the forceful catalyst that I needed to really put my gratitude practice on full blast.

In the thick of my anxiety episodes, I could hardly go an hour without my heart rate shooting up, my breathing becoming laborious, and my mind spinning. I couldn't shake the feeling that I was doing something wrong. The fact that I couldn't figure out *what* I was doing wrong only amplified my concerns. I decided, one October afternoon, in the middle of a spiral, that I just couldn't let this pattern continue. Isn't it crazy that sometimes we need these 'rock bottom' moments to really force us to take action?

I distinctly remember speaking aloud to myself, 'Sarah, there is nothing logical to be anxious about right now. Here are the facts that I have to prove this. You have an amazing family. You have amazing friends. You have a stable job (in an economy in which that is a gift), etc.'

It didn't take me long into this self—pep—talk to realize what it is I was doing. I was literally listing off all of the things that I am grateful for. I would be lying if I said that I didn't try to interrupt myself (rude) with the 'yeah, but...' comments. For example, my inner monologue may have sounded like 'Sarah, you have an amazing family and friends!' 'Yeah, but I don't have a boyfriend at 25, that's really weird.'

In my experience, I have realized that one of the hardest and most heartbreaking pieces of the human emotional experience is that we hyper—focus on the few things we don't 'have' while negating to realize and to acknowledge the bountiful blessings we do have.

Now, circling back to my take on 'practicing gratitude'. The act of practicing gratitude is *so much more* than just making a list of the good things in your life, as I once thought. The act of practicing gratitude is as integral a life skill as brushing our teeth. Literally, by speaking aloud to yourself the countless blessings you have, at least once a day, you are making the conscious choice to focus on your blessings and gifts in this life, which lay the foundation to continue working towards other pieces in your life that you may strive for.

Put it in your tool belt

Instead of a well-defined activity to leave you with after this chapter, I just want to challenge you. I want to challenge you to, literally, interrupt your anxiety with gratefulness. This will feel odd at first, know that. But, this will become habitual. By consciously interrupting your anxious inner monologue with a grateful undertone, you will be able to look at your stressors with a different perspective. Instead of hearing yourself say, 'I have this blessing, but I don't have this', you'll notice yourself saying 'I don't have this, but look at what I do have, and with this foundation, I will continue to grow.'

8
Show Up

This is one of the only chapters in this book that is about how we interact with each other, as opposed to solely how we speak to and about ourselves. It's certainly applicable in both respects (self talk and relationally), but this chapter will delve into the power of showing up for ourselves *and* others.

There is a quote I love and live by, originally said by Regina Brett. She stated, 'No matter how you feel, get up, dress up, and show up.'

This is such a powerful phrase to me. It's just two simple words, but carries SUCH meaning. Oftentimes, when things get tough, we have an instinct to recede and to bury our heads in the sand. I beg you, though, please never stop showing up. Show up for yourself. Show up to each day with your head held high. Show up ready to take on the day and make the world a better place. Just show up.

Not only do I challenge you to show up for yourself each and every moment of every day, I also challenge you to show up for others. If you think about it, that's all that we as humans really want and need from each other. We need people in our lives that will show up when it's good and will show up when life is hard. I am not only speaking literally & physically here — you don't need to travel far and wide to show up for someone! When I think of friends of mine who have embodied this tool the most, it's friends who simply take the time to ask how things are going and who *truly* want to know.

On that same token, I think that one of the simplest, yet most powerful, acts of friendship is to just reach out. Reach out to friends for no particular reason other than to check in. Think about when you get a text or a call from a friend, just because. How does that make you feel? There is, of course, no right answer to this question. I know that I personally feel cherished and valued, because someone went out of their way to reach out and tell me they're thinking of me. WHAT A GIFT.

PS, heck ya I got a tattoo that says 'show up'. Like I said, these two words carry such power in my life. I hope it does in yours, too.

Put it in your tool belt

How can you show up for yourself more in the next few days, weeks, months, years? How can you show up for others on that same timeline? The chart below is, of course, just a template. This is something that I challenge you to revisit often, and continue your practice of showing up for others and for yourself.

Who can I show up for?	What can I do for this person (brainstorming)?	Final idea/check when done!	
Myself!	*Remind myself that I am doing just fine on the 'timeline of life' and that I am right where I need to be.*	*A friend got a great promotion at work, which is exciting! It can be hard to see others progress faster than me, though. But I reminded myself that I will find the right opportunities for me, and that's unique to anyone else!*	✔

Who can I show up for?	What can I do for this person (brainstorming)?	Final idea/check when done!	

9
Stop Trying to Put the Puzzle Together

For so long, I had always pictured life as one big puzzle. Comprised of multiple pieces that fit together perfectly, it was my duty to complete each piece, place it where it belongs, and move on to another. That piece of the puzzle would be in its proper place. I'm laughing while I write this because this is one that is great in concept but, as the title of this chapter indicates, life is not a puzzle.

Here are some of the silly puzzle pieces I have tried to perfect.

- Once I finally finish my college degree, I'll be done with classroom learning forever and can put that puzzle piece in its place.
- Once I finally find the perfect group of friends, I would never have to worry about making friends or maintaining friendships.
- Once I finally nail down the perfect budget, I wouldn't have to think through my expenses each month.
- Once I finally perfect my workout regimen, I won't ever have to struggle with a lack of motivation to get to the gym and workout again.
- Once I finally figure out my career and 'life purpose', I'll be done with that piece of the puzzle and would never have to make a change again.
- Once my skin cleared up from acne, I'll never have to worry about anything with my appearance ever again!

Copy, paste.

Here's the thing though: life is not a puzzle, nor is it linear like I so naively thought. There will be times in your life and mine where we feel like we have secured one 'piece of the puzzle' and that we can move on completely. Life will not shy from reminding us, though, that all great things in life require work to maintain. The best relationships require both people to communicate openly and often. The best jobs require us to be lifelong learners and to continue to seek growth. The best workout regimens require us to continually push ourselves.

This may come as a surprise to some, but I actually *love* the fact that the best things in life require us to constantly work at it. How boring would life be if we just had one fitness goal one time and then coasted the rest of the time? The same line of thinking could be translated to friendships or other relationships! How boring would life be if we made a few good friends but never expanded our friend groups and refined our relationships? The answer to all of these examples is simple — it would be VERY boring.

Put it in your tool belt

What pieces of your life's puzzle have you been trying to 'secure'? Sunlight is the best disinfectant, and this is the perfect example of a time in which bringing these 'puzzle pieces' to light is the best way to see how silly they seem. These items in the leftmost column can be as simple as 'find the best pair of jeans', or it can be as complex as 'find the perfect work/life' balance. No puzzle piece is too small to be brought to light. Let's do it together! I'll start. *Hint: if the last column answer isn't 'yep' quite yet, that's okay!!*

Once I 'finally'...	Then...	Does that sound crazy yet?
Pay off that credit card debt	*I'll never have an issue with money or budgeting again.*	*Yep*

Once I 'finally'...	Then...	Does that sound crazy yet?

10
Look at Your Timeline and Laugh

I saw this concept shared online the other day and I haven't been able to stop thinking about it. In essence, just because people are getting things that you may want quicker than you doesn't mean that it's not possible for you, because your timeline is not the same as theirs. There is a reason why it's not coming into your life right now. There's a reason why you don't have this right now.

The other day I was thinking about how 15—year—old Sarah would feel about that life that 25—year—old Sarah is leading right now. I have caught myself doing this a few times recently, and cannot recommend this every once in a while. In an odd way, this practice forces me to really think through the steps in life that have gotten me to where I am today.

15—year—old Sarah would be SO confused why things didn't go according to plan. The plan was to go to nursing school, meet a husband there, get married, and work at a hospital (the maternity ward, in particular) while building a family and chasing the suburban dream. There was very little doubt in my mind, 10 years ago, that this plan would unfold without issue.

I am literally laughing as I type this because, I can only imagine that after 15—year—old Sarah calms down (she was a little bit high strung), she would be *so freaking excited* to hear about all of the things that happened in place of the 'original plan'. The change in majors while in school. The change in career after school. The skydiving adventure. The trips across the world. The trips across the country. The new friends. The new challenges.

The new triumphs. The new book written. The new hobbies. And then I would tell her about all of the plans I have for the next ten years and we can laugh about that together.

In all seriousness, though, I think it's important to look back and reflect on all that has happened, on a daily basis, weekly, annual, or over the course of 10 years, because life comes at us fast. The reality is that if my 'plan' had have panned out as I was so sure it was going to, lots of most treasured gifts and memories would not have been a possibility. If I had stayed in the education field (where my degree is), I would not have had the capability to pick up and travel to Colorado to work remotely for two weeks. That trip holds such dear memories, and I am forever grateful that my plan 'fell apart' for opportunities like this to be presented.

Of course, that two week trip to Colorado is just one example of an experience that would not have been possible if everything went according to plan. The truth of the matter is that we have NO idea how good things can be in our lives. Sure, it's fun to make plans and look forward to things. I'm in full support of that! If I've learned anything in the last quarter of a century on this big rock, though, it's that things happen for a reason. It may be 5 or 10 years before we can understand that reasoning, but I promise you they do. Plans fall apart for better plans to come together. Timelines get all screwed up from our perspective, so that we can look back in 10 years and see that it's all made sense.

Put it in your tool belt

Let's spend some time looking at your timeline over the course of the past 10 years or so. The prompts below will ask you to fill in the blanks to really delve into all that has happened in your life over the past 10 years. *Spoiler alert: It's going to be shocking.* I'll complete a few lines with my answers, to show how it should look. On the following pages, you'll see more blank prompts set up like these, because I do encourage you to do this for multiple periods of time (10 years, 1 year, 5 years, etc.).

My example

10 years ago, I was __*15*__ years old. At the time, I was __*in high school, planning which nursing school I would attend.*__

At that time, this is how I pictured my life 10 years from then. ***I was going to attend nursing school, and meet a husband there. After school, I would work as an RN or as even an NP and we would move to the suburbs and start a family, living the suburban dream.***

In reality, right now in life I am ***working in a corporate setting with an education degree under my belt, unmarried, with a lifetime of adventures already. I am currently training for a half marathon, and I live in the city in a one bedroom apartment that I have worked so hard to make a little slice of heaven.***

Takeaways/thoughts from this reflection: ***So much has happened to get me where I am today! I was set on having my 'plan' unfold as I wanted it to and I'm actually happy it didn't. I still have a long life ahead of me, and a lot of changes headed my way still. I'm excited!***

Your Turn

10 years ago, I was _____ years old. At the time, I was _____

(write a little bit about what you were doing in life at this point in time)

_____

_____.

At that time, this is how I pictured my life 10 years from then. _____

(write a little bit about what you thought you'd be doing in 10 years)

_____

_____.

In reality, right now in life I am _____

(write a little bit about where you're at in life right now)

_____

_____.

Takeaways/thoughts from this reflection: _____

(write a little bit about what you've noticed and observed from comparing your 'plan' to the 'reality')

_____

_____.

Your Turn
(enter your own age/year)

___ years ago, I was _____ years old. At the time, I was _____

(write a little bit about what you were doing in life at this point in time)

_____

_____.

At that time, this is how I pictured my life 10 years from then. _____

(write a little bit about what you thought you'd be doing in 10 years)

_____

_____.

In reality, right now in life I am _____

(write a little bit about where you're at in life right now)

_____

_____.

Takeaways/thoughts from this reflection: _____

(write a little bit about what you've noticed and observed from comparing your 'plan' to the 'reality')

_____

_____.

11

Find the Butterflies

Little known fact about Sarah Gifford — I am a plethora of random and awful jokes. Like, jokes so bad they're good. I also know a lot of really random, one—off facts that seemingly serve no purpose taking up space in my brain. BUT, listen to this one. Butterflies cannot see their own wings. Other butterflies can see them, and we can see them, but a butterfly cannot observe his or her own wings. This isn't really a fact, I guess, just an observation. Semantics.

Ironic, isn't it, that this is the piece of the butterfly that we admire most. Butterflies have zero idea how beautiful we see them. They have zero idea how we ooh and aah at their beauty, and how we marvel at their peaceful nature. To a butterfly, they are just beings flying in the air.

I would argue that the same is true about those of us that don't fly in the air. We have zero idea of the profound impact that we can have on others. Some days, we're just simply existing. What we don't realize, though, is how much simply our presence means to some people.

I have been trying to do a better job recently of telling people when they have an impact like this on me, because, like the butterfly, they may have no idea. I know that if by some chance I have this type of positive impact on people's lives and/or the world, I would want to know! There's this saying that I love, and although it's a bit morbid, I think it's a great reminder. "Everything we say at funerals should be said at birthday parties instead. We leave so much unspoken."

Put it in your tool belt

Instead of a well—defined activity, I want to challenge you to tell people when they're positively affecting your life. Tell people when they're making you feel happy or appreciated. I would venture to guess that you telling them of this will make them feel happy and appreciated, too. Feel free to use the space below to make little notes of reminders to tell people how much they mean to you!

Conclusion

Whether you are reading this as a middle schooler, a high schooler, a college aged young adult, a grandparent, or anywhere in—between, I know that you have made it through some *hard* days and some *hard* times. You have overcome so much, and you will continue to overcome so much. I am so proud of you. Take a minute right now, and think about some of your toughest times. Guess what, YOU DID IT! You made it through those times. Whether you can see it or not now, you grew so much over that time and through that journey.

Sometimes, when I am going through a hard time, I stop and remind myself of this. I am not going to lie and say that it makes me instantly feel better, but I do notice myself feeling a bit more hopeful once I realize this. I challenge you to do the same. Next time you find yourself feeling down, upset, anxious, or whatever it may be, remind yourself that you have been here before, this is not new territory, and you have overcome this before. If anything, you are better equipped to work your way through this now than you were in the past. You are stronger than you know, believe me.